My opposition to interviews lies in the fact that offhand answers have little value or grace of expression, and that such oral give and take helps to perpetuate the decline of the English language. **—James Thurber**

I get nervous when I do print interviews because I know that whatever I say is going to be shown through the lens of whomever I'm talking to. **—Emma Stone**

There's lots of interviews now where nobody seems to talk about anything. Like it's illegal. But it can be fun if you stay involved. Like most conversations.
—Imogen Poots

My wife thinks I should do interviews by listening to the questions and playing the answers on the guitar.
—David Gilmour

I've never really done any interviews as myself.
—Sacha Baron Cohen

I never turn down requests for interviews. **—Bob Ross**

I often conduct interviews in my truck.
—William Shatner

inter/views

CALUMET EDITIONS

Minneapolis MN

Printed in the United States of America
10 9 8 7 6 5 4 3 2 1
ISBN 978-1-950743-69-8

Cover art: Volodymyr Hryshchenko
Book layout & design: Stephan Shambert

inter/views

poems by

christopher chambers

contents

walter abish / neil jordan

This is not a film, it is a precise act of disbelief,
the figures Camus wrote about, all certainty having vanished.
He shortly thereafter commits suicide, as if to prove
he is doing nothing, and he yet is the center of everything.

The figures Camus wrote about, all certainty having vanished
as characters are, if anything, points of departure.
He did nothing, and he was the center of everything
and conveyed the dubiousness of the familiar.

Characters are, if anything, points of departure,
like quantum physics, Heisenberg, somebody typing
and conveying the dubiousness of the familiar,
faithful to the text, to arrive at these peculiar circumstances.

Like quantum physics, Heisenberg, or somebody, was typing.
He shortly thereafter committed suicide, as if to prove
faithful to the text, and arrive at these peculiar circumstances.
This is not a film, but a precise act of disbelief.

india amos / frank black

I've been trying to put lyrics on this one for years,
and I find that 4/4 just gets in my way sometimes
for a mix of aesthetic and technical reasons.
Nobody can tell it's there in the first place.

Sometimes I find that 4/4 just gets in my way,
so I arrange the text on a more consistent grid.
Though nobody can tell if it's there in the first place,
making it look better. Neater. More consistent. Less eccentric.

I arranged the text on a more consistent grid
—you should never rely on interviews as being factual—
to make it look better. Neater. More consistent. Less eccentric.
It's uncommon, elegant without being dainty.

I never rely on interviews with musicians as being factual
for a mix of aesthetic and technical reasons.
It is uncommon, elegant without being dainty and
I'd been trying to put lyrics on this one for years,

janine antoni / wendy wasserstein

I sit alone in a room in London and write this while
you are with something I have been intimate with.
I can't believe there is someone growing up in the next room
and yet I choose seduction over hostility.

You are with something I have been intimate with
at a point where I'm actually feeling the repercussions.
And yet I choose seduction over hostility and
begin this before swoon, but complete it afterwards.

At a point where I'm actually feeling the repercussions
the audience is the wild card, rocks from afar look married.
I begin right before swoon but complete it afterwards.
Conceptually your response was in keeping with

the audience, the wild card, rocks from afar looking married.
I can't believe there is someone growing up in the next room
though conceptually your response is in keeping with
me sitting alone in a room in London, writing this.

nicholson baker / madonna

I like putting myself in strange places and trying to survive—
it's the only structure I have, really, the only plot,
like French recordings floating in my subconscious.
I've always liked to inspect lichens at close range.

The only structure I have, really, the only plot
is trying to figure things out, gathering an infrastructure.
I've always liked to inspect lichens at close range,
combining them with some odd citation I've found

trying to figure things out, gathering an infrastructure.
I felt pleasure when I turned the lens a little bit,
combining it with some odd citation I found
while driving around, listening to half-formed tracks.

I feel pleasure when I turn the lens a little bit
with French recordings floating in my subconscious.
I drive around, listening to half-formed tracks
and put myself in a strange place, trying to survive.

roger boylan / cher

I was an outsider no matter what business I went into,
a journeyman specializing in electronic carillon bells.
Even in the mainstream, I was swimming up it.
Imagine Flaubert's lengthy missives through cyberspace.

A journeyman specializing in electronic carillon bells
even in old clothes, he is walking around smart.
Imagine Flaubert's lengthy missives through cyberspace,
no idea, just burning the candle at both ends.

Even in old clothes, he is walking around smart,
suffering, unable to run a marathon or afford a satellite dish.
I have no idea, just burning the candle at both ends now,
studying pub interiors, mostly, with time out for Irish history.

I suffer, not able to run a marathon or afford a satellite dish.
I return to whenever I can, especially, At-Swim-Two-Birds
to study pub interiors, mostly, with time out for Irish history.
I am still an outsider no matter what business I go into.

judy budnitz / david byrne

I have no idea what's going to happen next—
German electronic music, spicy food, a book by Faulkner or
sentences like the man in the dog suit whines outside my door.
I never listen to the radio unless I rent a car.

German electronic music, spicy food, a book by Faulkner
make me think about the subjectivity of memory, the paradox
that I never listen to the radio unless I rent a car.
There was no single spark. For a long time I'd been thinking

about the subjectivity of memory, the paradox of witness
but there's something that betrays it, there's a twist
There was no single spark. For a long time I'd been thinking,
doing things in parallel, not moving forward, tracing a line

but there's something that betrays it, there's a twist,
sentences like the man in the dog suit whines outside my door
doing things in parallel, not moving forward, tracing a line
so I have no idea what's going to happen next.

nick cave / r. crumb

I dream a lot, I go into my office and sit around
with a whole different set of cultural inputs.
I'm not one to reflect so I barrel onwards
with paper and pens and stationary supplies.

This is a whole different set of cultural inputs
and always feels difficult, never very healthy.
I like paper and pens and stationary supplies
and songs all growing out of the piano.

It always feels difficult, never very healthy,
months and months of labor every day
until the songs all grow out of the piano.
We all enjoy making a noise.

After months and months of labor every day
I'm not one to reflect so I barrel onwards
bcase we do all enjoy making a noise and
dreaming a lot, going into the office to sit around.

teresa leo /christopher chambers

These concepts are apparent in chaos and ecology theories.
This is the second time you've used the word amuse
positioned as a fulcrum between science and the sublime.
The secret is balancing the self and the self's response to Eno.

This is the third time you've used the word amuse—
are you inferring that society is ailing or lame?
The secret is balancing the self and the self's response to Eno,
forgiving this deranged syntax and ghosting of meaning.

Are you inferring that society is ailing or lame?
Will society come to respect the finite fragility of the Earth,
forgiving this deranged syntax and ghosting of meaning?
This describes the process pretty well, a recipe for disaster.

Can society come to respect the finite fragility of the Earth?
These appear to be two completely unrelated seriatum
describing the process pretty well, a recipe for disaster.
These concepts are apparent in chaos and ecology theories.

laura dern / ken foster

I wanted to go to Jupiter, that was my plan from day one,
I was curious, and perhaps a little concerned
that if you got hysterical you'd throw that dog out the window
rather than fluffing everything up with style.

I was curious, and perhaps a little concerned
that there are no accidents in what we end up doing.
Rather than fluffing everything up with style
we both ended up in my kitchen in Portland.

There were no accidents in what we ended up doing,
only a journey to darkness through light, or vice versa
both of us ending up in my kitchen in Portland,
revealing things that others might shy away from.

It's always a journey to darkness through light, or vice versa—
you get hysterical and throw the dog out the window
revealing things that others might shy away from.
I still want to go to Jupiter, that was my plan from day one.

sean dingle / larry king

There was DNA that led to this, I mean, the mind boggles,
vocals tapering into yelps, facial tics as the lines are forced out.
Forget fingerprints and the rest—that will come out in court.
Less obviously jaunty and erotic than ease on down the road,

vocals taper into yelps and facial tics as the lines are forced out.
And what was going through your head sitting in the car,
less obviously jaunty and erotic than ease on down the road?
Knowing about the wackos out west, in other parts, the crazies,

what was going through your head, sitting in the car
in diguises, chewing tobacco to the sounds of Merle Haggard?
You know all about the wackos out west, the crazies
looking tanned and quite healthy after weeks surfing?

In disguises, chewing tobacco to the sounds of Merle Haggard,
forget fingerprints and the rest. That will come out in court.
He was looking tanned and quite healthy after weeks surfing,
There was DNA that led to this, I mean, the mind boggles.

mike doughty / laura dern

I don't know what the whole story is there. No one does,
but the real benefit of these journeys is more abstract—
every person at the table has had a weird experience as a child,
in the traditional sense where two guys pass around a guitar.

But the real benefit of these journeys is more abstract.
It's about judgement and fear in a puritanical society
in the traditional sense where two guys pass around a guitar.
The sound is like a weird foam that fills up the frequency.

It's about judgement and fear in a puritanical society,
Cambodian nymphs from the walls of Ankor Wat,
a sound like weird foam that fills up the frequency,
and sexual frankness that never turns into hypocrisy.

Like Cambodian nymphs from the walls of Ankor Wat,
every person at the table has had a weird experience as a child,
and the sexual frankness never turns into hypocrisy.
I don't know what the whole story is here. No one does.

mike doughty / david lynch

I love the feeling in the air you catch of old Hollywood,
it's kind of an exotic date with myself, a hobby I've picked up.
There's no law against strangeness, it's just the context,
this razor sharp distinction between cool and uncool.

It's kind of an exotic date with myself, a hobby I've picked up.
You have to be in love with yourself, see these ideas unfolding,
a razor sharp distinction between cool and uncool.
At first it's rough, then little by little we get into that spot.

You have to be in love with yourself, see these ideas unfolding,
as opposed to soul coughing, which is a shitload of color.
At first it's rough, then little by little we get into that spot,
never like a melody or a lyric but like something integral

as opposed to soul coughing, which is a shitload of color.
There's no law against strangeness, it's just the context,
never like a melody or a lyric but something really integral.
I love the feeling in the air you catch of old Hollywood.

david fried / lili taylor

This is not art about art, nor is it a manifesto of what could be.
Eight pages into the script I break down. A door opens
and we find ourselves in bed with our own past and future.
Sometimes it's a fight about something I don't believe in.

Eight pages into the script she breaks down and a door opens.
She's clever enough to eat, sleep, and reproduce biologically.
Sometimes it's a fight about something I don't believe in.
I am happy we do not need to copy books by hand like monks.

At least clever enough to eat, sleep, and reproduce
biologically, and I know I'm Nate's friend from Seattle,
happy that I do not need to copy books by hand like monks.
I'd go so far as to carve his name in my forehead.

All I know is that I'm Nate's friend from Seattle,
and we find ourselves in bed with our own past and future
and I go so far as to carve his name in my forehead.
This is not art about art, nor is it a manifesto of what could be.

jorie graham / johnny depp

Jesus Christ sits before us in an alcove
trying to sell a gross or two of ballpoint pens.
Children run around, people kiss the veil, and all the rest.
I don't know when the show will end but I see it coming.

Trying to sell a gross or two of ballpoint pens
no doubt the easy, sunny glamour of it is everywhere.
I don't know when the show will end but I see it coming,
the book clicking shut, a feeling one just learns to recognize.

No doubt the easy, sunny glamour of it is everywhere,
John Waters swooping down from heaven like an angel.
The book clicks shut, a feeling one just learns to recognize—
and it's over, that's your ride, step to the right and fuck off.

John Waters swoops down from heaven like an angel,
children run around, people kiss the veil, and all the rest.
It's over, that's your ride, step to the right and fuck off
because Jesus Christ sits before us now in an alcove.

maggie gyllenhaal / robyn hitchcock

There are a couple of lines I just can't get my head around.
We'd pulled up all the carpet and polished the old floors.
I had taken out my contact lenses so I couldn't see
that we were quite fond of each other in our own unique way.

We'd pulled up all the carpet and polished the old floors.
I was in this suit and I didn't know where to put my hands
but we were quite fond of each other in our own unique way.
Once while traveling alone in Spain I met this couple,

I was in this suit and I didn't know where to put my hands.
Like a modern experimental atonal dissonant freaky whatever,
While traveling alone in Spain once, I met this couple
sinking into the parking lot known as middle age.

Like a modern experimental atonal dissonant freaky whatever
I had to take out my contact lenses so I wouldn't see
that we were sinking into the parking lot known as middle age.
There still are a couple of lines I just can't get my head around.

barry hannah / barbet schroeder

Even in a car wreck facts and time are rearranged
so that we revisit the story from another angle,
almost frantic to have a moment of clarity and peace,
or in Vallejo's words, a reality that becomes mad.

We must revisit the story from another angle.
Doomed to lengthy fragments, ghosts in the book,
Vallejo's words becoming a reality, madness,
the camera moving around us like in Hitchcock.

Doomed to lengthy fragments of a ghost in a book,
with consciousness of death and exuberance,
we live in an apartment in Mexico City, but always
it is less violent, technically, than an American movie.

And always conscious of death and exuberance,
almost frantic to have a moment of clarity and peace,
though less violent, technically than an American movie,
we witness the car wreck and rearrange the facts and time.

patty hearst / bram van moorhem

This is where it begins for me, right on this road.
You know, trouble is easy to find when you go looking for it,
assuming you aim for perfection through improvisation—
receipts, license plates, hand prints, palm prints, fingerprints.

You know trouble is easy to find when you go looking for it,
a clever way, a head start, determined to rock your world.
Receipts, license plates, palm prints, fingerprints—
we were hauled in as an exciting new classic biker gang.

It's a clever way, a head start to rock your world,
and I have to say it was a really liberating experience
when we were hauled in as an exciting new classic biker gang,
in terms of throwing down the gauntlet, saying look,

I have to say it was a really liberating experience.
Assume that you aim for perfection through improvisation
in terms of throwing down the gauntlet. Say look,
this is where it begins for me, right on this road.

steven holl / james casebere

Say a suburban white midwestern kid moves to New York
with his little drawings in a watercolor notebook.
Allow the viewer to step back from the experience
and the photograph may be a happy accident.

See the little drawings in the watercolor notebook—
goofy, childlike, handmade and playful.
The photograph was a happy accident,
reversing day and night, upstairs and downstairs.

Goofy, childlike, handmade and playful,
an anonymous poster thing in the Lower East Side
reverses day and night, upstairs and downstairs
to create a sense of wistful reverie, of memory.

The anonymous poster thing in the Lower East Side
allows the viewer to step back from the experience,
creates a sense of wistful reverie of the past, the memory of
a suburban, midwestern white kid who moved to New York.

michel houellebecq / lou reed

At the beginning, our hero makes commentaries on life
involved with feedback, guitars, playing with tape recorders,
as well as the insect on the carpet, the light bulb exploding.
He has a scar on his forehead he got dueling with Nietzsche.

Add feedback, guitars and playing around with tape recorders.
I had an image of it without actually ever having been there.
He has a scar on his forehead he got dueling with Nietzsche
or in conversation between our hero and the psychologist.

I had an image of it without actually ever having been there.
He introduced me to the idea of drone, playing with the speeds
of conversations with psychologists, echoes of interviews.
A bunch of drag queens shooting up, the heavy metal trip.

He introduced me to the idea of drone, playing with the speeds
as well as the insect on the carpet, the light bulb exploding,
and a bunch of drag queens shooting up, the heavy metal trip
that begins with our hero making commentaries on life.

matthew johnson / dorothy allison

Nothing is certain except death, violence, and stubbornness.
In the case of inanimate objects, it's bad; with songs it's good,
the romance dangerous, like the drunken suicidal glory I felt
when some girl told me Keith Richards was going to show up.

In the case of inanimate objects, it's bad. With songs it's good,
and I cycle in and out of being able to handle it at all.
Some girl told me Keith Richards was going to show up, maybe
fuck up completely, and still have a moment of perfect grace.

I cycle in and out of being able to handle this at all. If I had
a dollar for every time a kid shouts out white man at the door,
I could fuck up completely and still have a moment of grace.
I'm nihilistic in a friendly way. I love it when things go wrong.

A dollar for every time a kid shout out white man at the door,
for every dangerous romance, every drunken suicidal glory...I
feel nihilistic in a friendly way. I love it when things go wrong,
and nothing's certain except death, violence, and stubbornness.

charlie kaufman / rick moody

Remember what Benjamin said about texts?
I was reading Abélard and Héloise's letters at the time,
a vignette shaped as much by omission as by action,
with symbolism that is enormously heavy handed and funny.

I was reading Abélard and Héloise's letters at the time,
an obsessive-compulsive hack with scissors and a desire
for symbolism that is enormously heavy handed and funny.
The ending is way too complicated to even talk about—

an obsessive-compulsive hack with scissors and a desire
for the hotly sexual, but with a patina of high art to it also.
The ending is way too complicated to even talk about. I like
a computer program generating a random sequence—

it's hotly sexual but with a patina of high art to it also,
a vignette shaped as much by omission as by action or
a computer program generating a random sequence.
Just remember what Benjamin said about texts.

pagan kennedy / charlie kaufman

I became obsessed with some nineteenth-century spiritualist,
I set up an expectation and then went in another direction.
I'm fascinated with that and can't really tell you why.
Ultimately television did not welcome me.

I set up an expectation and then went in another direction
with people who are just flamboyantly eccentric.
Ultimately television did not welcome me—
pop culture analysis was like a hall of mirrors.

I was with people who were just flamboyantly eccentric,
and at that point I felt a chill run up my spine.
Pop culture analysis was like a hall of mirrors,
but the echo of the stuff that's been cut still remains.

At this point I feel a chill run up my spine.
Growing older I find myself less interesting,
I like the echo of the stuff that's been cut remaining
like an obsession with some nineteenth-century spiritualist.

yusef komunyaaka / bill frisell

A notebook at the bottom of a ladder with words, images,
places in the music where you don't know black or white—
it's reaching for that surprise, the blue note.
Certain songs have a new light suddenly shed on them,

places in the music where you don't know black or white.
With slightly different adjustments and emotional calibration,
certain songs have a new light suddenly shed on them
and make us think of America as a stolen paradise.

With slightly different adjustments and emotional calibration,
you hear these momentary flashes where it's exactly
what makes us think of America as a stolen paradise.
It's an amazing and weird back and forth (laughter),

where you hear these momentary flashes. And it's exactly
like reaching for that surprise, the blue note,
the amazing and weird back and forth (laughter) and
a notebook at the bottom of the ladder, words and images.

rem koolhaas / t. c. boyle

I feel a nostalgia for architecture as public art
and begin to wonder where these concepts originated—
preservation in Beijing, a department store for books,
withdrawing to create one's own utopia.

I began to wonder where this concept originated,
an emblem of serenity or an instrument of business,
no more withdrawing to create one's own utopia.
I like to call this new condition junk space,

once an emblem of serenity, now an instrument of business.
So forget dignity, or even sense. It's all over.
So let's call this new condition junk space
and try to move beyond positive and negative

forgetting dignity, or even sense. I'm over
the themes obsessed me from the beginning,
trying to move beyond positive and negative.
Yet I still feel a nostalgia for architecture as public art.

richard lindner / jason trachtenburg

I don't know what I'm talking about, but I feel very strongly
the sonic quality of a harmonic player is an unique approach
to doing things right now and fast and let's not talk about it.
It's a situation in which life becomes the act, we don't practice.

I need a harmonic player, an unique approach, somic quality
of watching children drawing on the pavement delighted.
It's a situation in which life becomes the act. We don't practice
a message of the eye, a poetic approach to let the colors go.

I watch children drawing on the pavement, delighted
to have the history of rock and roll in my consciousness,
a message of the eye, a poetic approach to let the colors go,
like cellular phones or the politics of nutrition.

With the history of rock and roll in my consciousness,
I go out and look in an ashcan and say this is beauty,
like cellular phones or the politics of nutrition.
I don't know what I'm talking about, but I feel very strongly.

peter markus & richard hell

What I discovered early on is that God is just a sound,
a muse, or the collective unconscious. I'm just paraphrasing
that scene at the end of the story with the hammer and nails.
I do believe there is a husk that time whistles through.

I'm just paraphrasing, a muse, or the collective unconscious,
working out some sort of Dr. Jekyll / Mr. Hyde tension,
believing there is a husk that time whistles through.
I suppose I find comfort in the repetition

working out some sort of Dr. Jekyl/Mr. Hyde tension.
I have no nostalgia for the past, for punk, any of that,
but I suppose I find comfort in the repetition
when there's a fair amount of incident, thousands of miles.

I have no nostalgia for the past, for punk, any of that,
that scene at the end of the story with the hammer and nails—
there's a fair amount of incident, and thousands of miles.
That is the challenge after discovereding God is just a sound.

thomas mcguane / johnny depp

Of course I have seen all the pirate movies
because you can make strange things happen at sea.
I was about three pages in and I knew this had to be made.
In an essentially nasty society like ours, certain disruptions

can make strange things happen, you see. You are better
off in a barn with a bottle of wine, quoting Poe,
in an essentially nasty society like ours. Certain disruptions:
uncontrollable rage and tears and joy all in like ten seconds.

Off in a barn with a bottle of wine, quoting Poe,
I would long to fly a long black banner from my boat
with uncontrollable rage and tears and joy all in ten seconds.
Then there would be back slapping and congratulations.

I would like to fly a long black banner from my boat.
I was about three pages in and I knew this had to be made,
and that there would be back slapping and congratulations
because of course I have seen all the pirate movies.

hermine meinhard / frank black

At a certain point language will start to form, magnetic filings
recorded live to stereo or mono. The challenge of capturing
short, fragmented lines in a jagged landscape
is more pleasurable than a facsimile of live performance.

We record live to stereo or mono. The challenge of capturing
a piece of lightning was one of the very first
and more pleasurable than a facsimile of live performance
related to my predilection for surprising leaps.

A piece of lightning was one of the very first,
but the fact is I'd been driving through Llano for years
in relation to my predilection for surprising leaps.
What UFO references? There may be a couple, but

the fact is I'd been driving through Llano for years,
past short, fragmented lines in the jagged landscape.
There may be a couple UFO references but
at a certain point language starts to form magnetic filings.

rick moody / wendy wasserstein

I wanted to do something where play was my motive.
A play, like old money, can go in many directions,
hijacking sounds floating around in Western culture.
There is a point where I'm actually feeling the repercussions.

A play, like old money, can go in many directions,
moving toward more density and higher volume of sources.
There is a point where I'm actually feeling the repercussions,
in the same way hip hop and electronica are contemporary.

I moved toward more density and higher volume of sources.
She had been a dancer and she still wore leather pants,
in the same way hip hop and electronica are contemporary.
Yeah, it has a bad rap but I like that it has a bad rap.

She is a dancer and she wears leather pants,
hijacking sounds floating around in Western culture.
Yeah, she has a bad rap but I like that she has a bad rap,
and she's doing something where play is her motive.

stewart o'nan / neil young

I got burned out somewhere around Albuquerque
crosscutting between times or changing first and third
with a little transistor radio up to my ear.
It starts at the beginning of the next scene,

crosscutting between times or changing first and third,
big and rambling and gutsy and rhetorical.
It starts at the beginning of the next scene
where I spread the narrative consciousness,

big and rambling and gutsy and rhetorical.
That makes it possible to have the droning sound
that spreads the narrative consciousness.
It's not a specific town so much as a feeling

that makes it possible to have that droning sound
with the little transistor radio up to my ear.
It was not a specific town so much as the feeling
that I got burned out somewhere around Albuquerque.

robert pollard / guillermo arriaga

Of course it goes fast forward. It comes and goes like
little pictures of clusters of guys who look like rock bands
trying to create images without any flesh.
The advantage is that I have created my own world,

little pictures of clusters of guys who look like rock bands
and a dog like the dog in the story, an ordinary dog.
The advantage is that I have created my own world
like Gold Star for Robot Boy, I am a Scientist, and so on.

A dog like the dog in the story, an ordinary dog
is a pretty fucking powerful look at life and death.
Gold Star for Robot Boy, I am a Scientist, and so on.
I had a lot of time to think, driving across Texas,

taking a pretty fucking powerful look at life and death.
I tried to create images without any flesh.
I had a lot of time to think, driving across Texas.
Of course it goes fast forward, it comes and it goes.

mark richard / tom waits

I'm still looking for the ultimate sound of stress metal clang—
it's a need to construct a world in which I am God.
You're responsible for navigating through strange places,
some odd little snippet of a scene passing by a car window.

It's a need to construct a world in which I am God,
a throwaway line that I hear in passing, two strangers talking,
some odd little snippet of a scene passing by a car window.
You have to share a common desire for mystery and danger,

a throwaway line you hear in passing, two strangers talking.
all the while developing a crude shorthand or hieroglyphics.
You have to share a common desire for mystery and danger.
It begins with sounds and then the visual world comes second,

developed from a crude shorthand or hieroglyphics.
You're responsible for navigating through strange places,
beginning with sounds and the visual world coming second.
I'm still looking for the ultimate sound of stress metal clang.

gary sinese / samuel mockbee

You're lost, you get a phone call, you can't hardly carry on.
I play Rosencrantz, while you play Guildenstern
as if every stroke had meaning, a structural reason
that sends everybody into a frenzy.

I play Rosencrantz and you play Guildenstern
because the half-life is longer that way,
and sends everybody into a frenzy
like a kid on a bicycle, like the taste of blood.

The half-life is longer, like the way
I begged you for two months,
like a kid on a bicycle tasting her first taste of blood.
We tended towards gut-level realism, and fear.

I begged you for two months,
my paramount concern the push and pull of light and shadow,
the tendency towards gut-level realism, the fear
I'm lost, I'll get a phone call, and I won't be able to carry on.

patti smith / gordon lish

I understand the authority of that exultation, Let's get lost,
a collective hysteria I learned from reading about people,
unbudgeable acmes of expression in the language on my mind.
His voice was like a motorcycle through a cornfield,

a collective hysteria I learned from reading about people,
some kind of reply to the incommensurable insult of death.
His voice was like a motorcycle through a cornfield
and that's the only kind of shopping mall I want to be in.

My reply to the incommensurable insult of death
is a telegram I sent. Light and energy enclosed—
now that's the only kind of shopping mall I want to be in.
I made a couple of references, oblique things to show I knew,

and I sent a telegram: Light and energy enclosed
something at its best, both pleasurable and inspiring.
I made a couple of references, oblique things to show
I understand the authority of exultation. Now let's get lost.

audrey tatou / thomas mcguane

I'd like some muscles. Look at these arms!
I would hang from a roof to watch people fucking.
Oh yes, it's international, lots of trouble and constant drama,
looking for typography rather than veins.

I would hang from a roof to watch people fucking
in a lingerie ad, or undressing, or standing facing a wall.
We look for typography rather than veins,
everyone nice, everyone honest, and always disillusioned.

In a lingerie ad, or undressed and standing facing a wall,
I feel some sort of presence, the power-to-weight ratio
with everyone nice, everyone honest, and always disillusioned.
The really unforgiveable sin is to go on too long.

I feel some sort of presence, a power-to-weight ratio
(oh yes, it's international), lots of trouble and constant drama,
the unforgiveable sin of having gone on too long.
I'd like some muscles. Look at these arms!

lili taylor / jorie graham

My first typewriter was an Olivetti with a bullet hole in it.
I let it move through me, not easy, I keep getting in the way
of my sexy, highly exportable American attention span.
They are looking to go in the direction of...subtext: pretty.

I let it move through me, not easy, I kept getting in the way of
the glances not returned across the courtyard outside school.
They were looking to go in the direction of...subtext: pretty.
I was yet another soul added to the massive pile of soul debris.

Their glances were not returned across the courtyard.
I want to learn. I want a best friend who is Courtney Love.
I am yet another soul added to the massive pile of soul debris.
Oh my God! (laughs) I have demons, obviously.

I want to learn. I want to have a friend who is Courtney Love,
I want a sexy, highly exportable American attention span.
Oh my God! (laughter) I have demons, and obviously
my first typewriter was an Olivetti with a bullet hole in it.

hunter s. thompson / courtney love

I work my ass off, I deliver the goddamn goods and will again.
It's about using words to an end, and the Book of Revelation.
The Joycean argument about my typing skills is hysterical,
like drinking gasoline. It is the rage that taps the vein.

It's about using words to an end, and the Book of Revelation.
So there's that, the energy reaching in, part of one's divinity
drinking gasoline. It was the rage that tapped the vein,
screaming, kicking the walls, broken fax machines and phones.

So there's that, the energy reaching into part of one's divinity.
I was in a house in New Orleans watching the funeral on TV,
screaming, kicking the walls, broken fax machines and phones.
The history of this is instructive, a maudlin, truthless affair.

I was in a house in New Orleans watching his funeral on TV.
My keyboard was sticky, my angle was irony. I'm not a clerk.
The history of this is instructive, a maudlin, truthless affair.
I worked my ass off, I delivered the goods and will again.

jason trachtenburg / cindy sherman

Everywhere you look, people are talking about appropriation.
I had tried everything, for years I had been getting nowhere,
and by then it seemed like a thing, a real presence.
Then by accident I bought a slide projector for five dollars.

I tried everything, for fifteen years. I was getting nowhere
so I started using color but the printing was more expensive
and by accident I bought a slide projector for five dollars.
Me, me, me, mine is my mantra. The rest is just image making.

I started using color and the printing was more expensive,
but I'd been conditioned to turn everything into a song.
Me, me, me, mine is my mantra. The rest is just image making,
and carrying two projectors, backup lenses, backup bulbs.

I'd been conditioned to turn everything into a song,
and by then it seemed like a thing, a real presence.
I always carry two projectors, backup lenses, backup bulbs and
everywhere I look, people are talking about appropriation.

sergio vega / simon winchester

There is an evanescent trail people draw through genealogy.
I say we give them microphones right now.
It is clearly a fugue state, chemical in nature,
arguments, fights, brothel visiting, drunkenness, dueling.

I say we give them microphones right now.
Between Tarzan movies and the mambo band rehearsing,
arguments, fights, brothel visiting, drunkenness, dueling,
I was immersed in Dante. I cast a replica of his death mask

between Tarzan movies and the mambo band rehearsing.
A typical travel book, nicely reviewed, goes nowhere.
Immersed in Dante as I was, I cast a replica of his death mask
using words of East Indian origin like caravan and bungalow.

A typical travel book, nicely reviewed, and going nowhere,
is clearly a fugue state, chemical in nature,
evoking words of East Indian origin like caravan, bungalow—
the evanescent trail people draw through genealogy.

eliot wilson / nick cave

Sometimes I like to do it differently
but I always seem to buy the same clothes.
I keep going into this place, this little room
where some vestige of Romantic ideology lingers.

I always seem to buy the same clothes
hoping for a real freedom of sound and rawness
where some vestige of Romantic ideology lingers.
There was a song for a beautiful French film and

hope for a real freedom of sound and rawness
but I threw it to one side of the piano.
There was a song for a beautiful French film,
accessing stark industrial images, the stuff of war and loss.

I threw it to one side of the piano too.
I keep going into this place, this little room
to access to stark industrial images, the stuff of war and loss.
Sometimes I like to do it differently.

tom waits / jenny diski

We have these very haunting pages
intent on the sounds of an interior world—
whiteness and emptiness, that's the space.
That chair will disappear and things will emerge.

Intent on the sounds of an interior world,
we like minor keys down here. The light is different,
the chair disappears, and new things emerge.
What happened to that trumpet?

We like minor keys down where the light is different.
Do you know what Andy Warhol said?
I thought we had a trumpet in this thing.
Yes, yes, still the world goes around.

Did you know that Andy Warhol said
whiteness and emptiness is the space,
yes, yes. Still the world goes around
us and these very haunting pages.

sandra oh / michael martone

Sometimes I think my entire life I've been wearing a costume—
it helps me understand myth, it helps me understand symbol
which isn't easy—in fact, it turns out to be almost impossible.
You just can't do it with CGI or on an Los Angeles backlot.

It helps you understand myth and the symbolism
of a psychological disorder where one is prone to these delusions.
You just can't do it with CGI or on an Los Angeles backlot or
eating sandwiches, playing Atari on Highway 61 Revisited.

It's a psychological disorder where one is prone to delusions.
I have no free time and I can't comment on academia
eating sandwiches, playing Atari on Highway 61 Revisited.
We're a nation where you can't be who you are forever

I have no free time and I can't comment on academia
which isn't easy—in fact, it turns out to be almost impossible
in a nation where you can't be who you are forever.
I sometimes think my entire life I've been wearing a costume.

professor mason writes the young poet
(a correspondence)

dear maddox

There is one which begins: observe how he negotiates his way,
not in scope and depth and comprehension of man on earth
as I intimated yesterday, in a stroke of self-obliteration.
One in which blackness, lack of color, is full and not paled.

Not in scope and depth and comprehension of man on earth
does a figure (the name of which I do not recollect)
begin in blackness, lack of color, both full and not paled.
In the theater banister is a noun and it cannot be wrinkled.

A figure, the name of which I do not recollect. Oxymoron?
Of course Milton coined darkness visible which is special.
In the theater banister is a noun and it cannot be wrinkled.
I am fond of talking about my image in the shop window glass

and of course Milton coining darkness visible was special.
As I intimated yesterday in a stroke of self-obliteration
I'm fond of talking about my image in the shop window glass,
an image which begins by observing how I negotiate my way.

dear maddox

The reader is likely to be fairly well impressed at first,
carried away too fast in a purely native direction.
It would be helpful to study the beginning of this, her solo.
It corresponds to voltage, like the nature (or quality).

He has been carried away too fast in a purely native direction.
Consciousness is electrical, the conductor is language—
it corresponds to voltage, like nature or quality,
the whole body articulated by syntax, rhetoric, and so forth.

Consciousness is electrical, and the conductor is language
I reckon. In the Swinburne category of verse writers
the whole body is articulated by syntax, rhetoric, and so forth,
possibly to find out who it is that her represents.

I reckon in the Swinburne category of verse writers
it would be helpful to study the beginning of this, her solo,
to possibly find out who it is that her represents.
The reader is likely to be fairly well impressed, at first.

dear maddox

There is little evidence of this except knowledge of mythology,
incantation and chant with the benefit of classical meters
molded by the voice of a particular and distinguished speaker.
How do I know this? I don't, quite. But neither did Montaigne.

Incantation and chant with the benefit of classical meters—
nowadays he will presumably let his lawyer make it for him.
How do I know this? I don't, quite. But neither did Montaigne.
There are fourteen or fifteen occurrences of the word she.

nowadays he will presumably let his lawyer make it for him,
all vague, and maybe mysterious, and probably phony.
There are fourteen or fifteen occurrences of the word she,
and the eternal footman holding her coat, snickering.

All vague, and maybe mysterious, and probably phony,
molded by the voice of a particular and distinguished speaker,
that old eternal footman holding her coat, snickering.
There is little evidence except the knowledge of mythology.

dear maddox

You will be able to transmit very little of my letter yesterday
with trust and the least violence, making the stranger friend,
and in the fullness of this utterance, the ear of the writer is
surely nothing like his work with titles like High Dive.

With trust and the least violence, make the stranger friend.
Read the poems of Ivor Winters who died last year
and consider his work with titles like High Dive,
alike in being meaningless, I would say. It is pretty hard

to read the poems of Ivor Winters who died last year.
Squash in Blossom, The Orb Weaver, and one called Swimmer,
alike in being meaningless. I would say it is pretty hard.
How mar blackness? How does the participle enacted work?

Squash in Blossom, The Orb Weaver, and one called Swimmer,
and in the fullness of his utterance, the ear of the writer
asks how mar blackness? How the participle enacted works.
You will be able to transmit very little of my letter yesterday.

dear maddox

And surely you know about Ransom and Tate.
Your own reflections doing very well, I believe,
though less impressive in the complimentary sense.
The writer's facility of the use of poetical stuff

in your own reflections does very well, I believe,
perhaps beyond rightness: better than rightness.
The writer's facility of the use of poetical stuff,
a gift that he should learn to take right advantage of,

is perhaps beyond rightness: better than rightness.
A little of the poetical is tolerable in poems,
a gift that he should learn to take right advantage of.
I will write more later if I can see the way to go.

Yes, a little of the poetical is tolerable in poems,
if it is possible to find out who it is he represents.
I will write more later if I can see the way to go,
for surely you know about Ransom and Tate.

dear maddox

I cannot imagine what he has been reading
with benefit of mind and the rhythms of English speech.
He searches the full unblemished darkness
sometimes not helpfully, and sometimes hurtfully.

With benefit of mind and the rhythms of English speech
this is his solo, friends and relatives,
sometimes not helpfully, and sometimes hurtfully
the pale comes to marred, and the marred to imperfection.

This is his solo, friends and relatives,
to swell progress, he starts a scene or two,
the pale coming to marred, and the marred to imperfection.
There are a good many words that fill up verses,

swelling progress, starting a scene or two,
for black is black without the benefit of full.
There are a good many words that fill up verses,
and I cannot imagine what he has been reading.

acknowledgments

The author acknowledges first publication of earlier versions of the following and thanks these anthologies and magazines and their discerning editors.

ART:MAG
"Tom Waits / Jenny Diski"

BlazeVOX
"Maggie Gyllenhaal / Robyn Hitchcock"
"Barry Hannah / Barbet Schroeder"
"Jorie Graham / Johnny Depp"
"Michel Houellebecq / Lou Reed"

Denver Quarterly
"Dear Maddox"
"Charlie Kaufman / Rick Moody"

Indiana Review
"Teresa Leo / Christopher Chambers"
"Jason Trachtenberg / Cindy Sherman"
"Gary Sinese / Samuel Mockbee"

near South
"Janine Antoni / Wendy Wasserstein"

Ninth Letter
"Hunter S. Thompson / Courtney Love"
"Nicholson Baker / Madonna"

Red Mountain Review
"India Amos / Frank Black
"Mike Doughty / Laura Dern"
"Barry Hannah / Barbet Schroeder"
"Peter Markus / Richard Hell"
"Lili Taylor / Jorie Graham"

Umpteen Ways of Looking at a Possum: Critical and Creative
Responses to Everette Maddox
"Dear Maddox"

Western Humanities Review
"David Fried / Lili Taylor"
"Patti Smith / Gordon Lish"

Christopher Chambers is the author of *Delta 88* and *Best Western*, two books of short fiction, and is co-editor with Peyton Burgess of the anthology *Ice Fishing with Alligators* (Calumet Editions 2021.) His work has appeared widely in literary magazines including *The Normal School*, *The Southern Review*, *Lit*, *Washington Square*, *Ninth Letter*, and *BOMB Magazine*. He works as a freelance editor and spends time in New Orleans, Milwaukee and Madison, Wisconsin.